THE FACTS ON
UFO'S
AND OTHER
SUPERNATURAL
PHENOMENA

John Ankerberg
& John Weldon

D1636958

HARVEST HOUSE PUBLISHERS
Eugene, Oregon 97402

Other books by
John Ankerberg and
John Weldon

The Facts on Astrology
The Facts on Creation vs. Evolution
The Facts on the Faith Movement
The Facts on False Teaching in the Church
The Facts on Hinduism
*The Facts on Holistic Health
and the New Medicine*
The Facts on Islam
The Facts on the Jehovah's Witnesses
The Facts on Jesus the Messiah
The Facts on Life After Death
The Facts on the Masonic Lodge
The Facts on the Mind Sciences
The Facts on the Mormon Church
The Facts on the New Age Movement
The Facts on the Occult
The Facts on Rock Music
The Facts on Roman Catholicism
The Facts on Sex Education
The Facts on Spirit Guides
*The Facts on UFO's and
Other Supernatural Phenomena*

**THE FACTS ON UFOS AND OTHER
SUPERNATURAL PHENOMENA**

Copyright © 1992 by The Ankerberg
   Theological Research Institute
Published by Harvest House Publishers
Eugene, Oregon 97402

ISBN 0-89081-991-2

CONTENTS

The UFOs Are Real

SECTION ONE
Introduction to UFOs

SECTION TWO
UFOs and the Occult

Conclusion
Notes

The UFOs Are Real

UFOs actually exist in some form; 5 to 10 percent of all UFO sightings remain truly unidentified.[1] Yet almost all serious researchers who have examined the subject are baffled by it. As Dr. J. Allen Hynek, a former UFO skeptic who headed the 18-year Air Force investigation, *Project Blue Book* commented, "The UFO phenomenon is the outstanding strange dilemma of our age. We don't know *what* they are."[2]

We think we do, and in this booklet we will tell you why.

The most commonly believed theory among those who accept UFOs is that UFOs represent incredibly advanced civilizations from outer space which are seeking to study, influence, and eventually contact humankind. Other theories suggest that UFO sightings are the result of misunderstandings of natural phenomena, deliberate hoaxes, psychological explanations, etc. But all these theories actually fail to explain the facts of the UFO phenomenon.

Yet millions of people continue to report sightings and tens of thousands report "close encounters" with UFOs. Around the world, several hundred million people now believe that UFOs are real. In fact, no one who has studied this subject can logically deny that the UFOs are slowly and deliberately exposing themselves to the entire world.[3] No nation is free of UFO reports, and many major nations around the world have officially or secretly engaged in serious investigations of UFOs at the governmental/military level. Indeed, "there are persistent rumors that highly placed officials in the U.S. government have long had evidence that another form of intelligence was contacting us."[4]

In the U.S. alone, tens of millions of dollars have been spent in official UFO investigations by the CIA, FBI, U.S. Army Intelligence, Naval Intelligence, and other organizations. Lawsuits filed under the Freedom of Information Act prove this in spite of the denials by such agencies.[5] In addition, literally tens of thousands of additional documents are being withheld in the name of national security, at a level of classification allegedly "two steps higher than information about the hydrogen bomb."[6]

It would appear that UFOs have been a topic of great concern and intensive secret research by other governments as well. For example, many years ago the French Minister of Defense, Robert Galley, publicly stated that the number of reliable UFO landing-occupant reports in his country was "very great" and "quite disturbing."[7] In fact, "The ubiquitous UFO phenomenon . . . [is] a phenomenon that has caused grave concern at high levels of many of the world's governments, despite their statements to the contrary."[8]

Polls consistently reveal that approximately 40 percent of Americans believe that UFOs are real.[9] Some leading researchers are stating even now that the alleged abductions of people by UFOs has reached "epidemic" proportions.[10]

Whatever one thinks about UFOs, no one can deny an important fact: Whether myth or reality, UFO phenomena and even the mere idea of UFOs have in the last 40 years had sizable influence on mankind.

Why are we qualified to write on the subject of UFOs? Coauthor John Weldon is the author of two previous books on the subject. In the past 20 years we have read, in part or full, hundreds of serious texts and hundreds more articles from professional journals on UFOs. We have talked with those who have seen UFOs, those who claim to have been abducted by UFOs, and those who claim to be in contact with UFO entities. We have examined the publications of the scientific or research-oriented civilian organizations and some of the declassified military documents, the skeptical literature, scores of "contactee" books, and the literature from what is probably the world's leading UFO journal, the British *Flying Saucer Review*, which has been in continuous publication since 1955.

After 20 years the extent and depth of our research now constitutes for us a conclusion that has become a virtual certainty: that UFOs constitute a spiritistic (demonic) phenomenon. We believe that such a conclusion may affect us all.

Of course, not everyone can easily accept such a hypothesis. But now is not the time for closed minds. Robert Galley, the former French Minister of Defense officially involved in UFO investigation, stated, ". . . my own profound belief is that it is necessary to adopt an extremely open-minded attitude toward these phenomena."[11]

Dr. Hynek and astrophysicist Dr. Jacques Vallee also assert, "The UFO phenomenon calls upon us to . . . approach boldly the edge of our accepted reality, and by mentally battering at these forbidding boundaries, perhaps open up entirely new vistas."[12] ". . . We need to line up all the things that a viable theory needs to explain [concerning UFOs]; . . . is there a hypothesis, no matter how strange, that explains the facts?"[13]

We believe there is.

SECTION ONE

Introduction to UFOs

1. What are UFOs?

UFOs are strange aerial phenomena that puzzle everyone. Most people think either that they are myths or that they represent the beginning phases of what will eventually prove to be contact with advanced forms of life from outer space. Indeed, UFO reports today are increasingly associated with strange "entities"—beings that some people also believe represent advanced life forms from deep in space.

The UFO phenomenon encompasses a wide range of phenomena and experiences. For purposes of simplification in describing these phenomena, we will use a broad classification incorporating the following seven categories:

- Distant Sightings (DS) involve observations of anomalous lights in the sky, nocturnal disks, etc., visually or on radar.

- Close Encounters of the First Kind (CEI) constitute sighting a UFO, with or without occupants, at 500 feet or closer.

- Close Encounters of the Second Kind (CEII) involve UFOs that leave physical effects on the environment such as landing marks, broken tree limbs, etc.

- Close Encounters of the Third Kind (CEIII) comprise the sighting of UFOs with occupants, at very close range, including landed craft with occupants in or about the craft.

- Close Encounters of the Fourth Kind (CEIV) involve alleged abductions by UFOs, where people claim to be involuntarily taken on board a UFO for experimentation, purposes of communication, or other reasons. Such episodes are characteristically "forgotten" until a strange series of events leads to "uncovering" the "abduction" under hypnosis.

- Close Encounters of the Fifth Kind (CEV) involve what are termed "contactees," those persons who claim to be in personal contact with UFO entities, typically through occult means.

- Close Encounters of the Sixth Kind (CEVI) include injuries or deaths resulting from a UFO close encounter.*

UFO phenomena are so complex that one leading researcher has advocated a 20-point classification system in order to better analyze the information.[14] Nevertheless, the solution to the UFO mystery cannot be found where most people look for it—distant sightings or CE I-III categories. The events do not contain enough data to properly understand what is behind modern UFOs. Rather, the solution is found in the key "close contact" categories (CE IV–VI). Why? Because it is here that genuine details emerge concerning the nature and purpose of the UFO phenomena and the entities that accompany it.

2. How are UFOs impacting mankind?

Few people realize the collective impact that UFOs have had on not just America but the entire world.

For example, shortly after the first modern sightings of UFOs began in 1947, television programs were inspired to popularize the idea of UFOs, aliens, interstellar travel, etc. Just a few of the dozens of major series include "The Adventures of Superman," "The Twilight Zone," "My Favorite Martian," "Star Trek," "Mork & Mindy," "Buck Rogers," "Alien Nation," etc.

Even in the field of TV cartoons ("The Masters of the Universe," "Captain Planet and the Planeteers") themes of outer space and contact with alien life have fascinated millions of children.

Consider the generation prior to the first UFO sightings, the period between 1920 and 1947. In this period there were less than a dozen science fiction movies relating to themes of UFOs and extraterrestrials. But from 1950 to 1980, well over a hundred such films have been produced. Among them are such classics as "The Day the Earth Stood Still," "The War of the Worlds," "2001: A Space Odyssey," "The Andromeda Strain," "Star Wars," "Close Encounters of the Third Kind," "Alien," "ET: The Extraterrestrial," and "Cocoon."[15]

---

* This is our own classification, modeled after the CEI-III typology originated by Dr. J. Allen Hynek.

This social fascination with alien themes is one reason why one of the world's leading UFO researchers, French astrophysicist Dr. Jacques Vallee, comments, "Over the past 20 years [the extraterrestrial alien] has assumed a powerful persona, so much so that expectations are now high that he actually exists among us...."[16]

Award-winning author Whitley Strieber, who has personally experienced harrowing contact with alleged UFO entities, claims that these strange and terrifying beings "are already having a staggering but largely hidden impact on our society, and their presence should be taken with the utmost seriousness."[17] Dr. Vallee himself refers to UFOs as "a bizarre, seductive, and often terrifying phenomenon reported by many witnesses as contact with an alien form of intelligence."[18]

Today, whatever people may have concluded concerning UFOs, the vast majority of mankind has heard about them. But what most people haven't heard is that they are dangerous. Serious UFO literature is replete with cases of physical, psychological, and spiritual harm resulting from UFO contact, whether such contact is sought out or not. Although it is not well-known, some people have even died following contact with UFOs or their alleged occupants.

UFO expert Dr. Jacques Vallee also observes, "The experience of a close encounter with a UFO is a shattering physical and mental ordeal. The trauma has effects that go far beyond what the witness recalls consciously. New types of behavior are conditioned, and new types of beliefs are promoted. The social, political, and religious consequences of the experience are enormous if they are considered, not in the days or weeks following the sighting, but over the timespan of a generation."[19]

Are UFO sightings and experiences common? It is only by examining the history of the phenomenon since 1947, the recently declassified documents under the Freedom of Information Act, and the publications of the leading civilian organizations in 20 countries around the world that we begin to comprehend some of the magnitude of the phenomenon. It strains credulity to believe that organizations such as the CIA, State Department, National Security Agency, FBI, Army, Navy, Air Force, and Defense Intelligence Agency would spend decades and vast amounts of resources in studying a nonexistent phenomenon.

The combination of sightings, Close Encounte abductions, and contactee phenomena is anyt significant, especially in light of the moderr contact with highly evolved and advanced F benevolent entities who could allegedly save our planet from destruction.

Indeed, around the world there is now widespread hope and support for contact with alien life. Even in the scientific community there is an extensive search for extraterrestrial life called SETI—the Search for Extraterrestrial Intelligence. At least half a dozen scientific undertakings are already underway attempting to "listen" for extraterrestrial communications in order to establish contact with them. In fact, "in 27 years of searching, 48 searches have been made from seven countries, mostly in radio wavelengths" which represent tens of thousands of hours of observation.[20] But on October 12, 1992, to celebrate the five-hundredth anniversary of Columbus' discovery of America, NASA, America's space agency, plans to begin the largest radio telescope search for extraterrestrial life in history. "In just the first 60 seconds, NASA will investigate more intensively than in all previous searches combined."[21]

That UFOs are real is no myth. That we are searching for signs of intelligent life in the universe, sometimes even desperately, is no myth. What *is* a myth is the idea of human evolution extended into the myth of cosmic evolution, and by implication a plurality of inhabited worlds which provides the expectation of UFO visits and eventual contact. However improbable, this outcome is deemed possible by a large number of people, among them influential scientists and politicians who are increasingly anxious about the endangered condition of our world.

Sociologist David Swift of the University of Hawaii observes that the underlying message of the UFO phenomenon is clear—that the creators of this "awesome object" (the UFO) have incredible knowledge and power. He concedes the common hope that such knowledge and power might be applied toward helping humanity solve its universal problems. "This is an alluring message, and it will become more attractive with each failure of conventional attempts to solve our complex problems. The thought of salvation from the sky is likely to grow in appeal."[22]

But the UFO phenomenon simply does not behave like extraterrestrial visitors. It actually *molds* itself in order to fit a given culture. Their purpose is not open contact, in the sense that we would expect friendly contact from advanced civilizations in space. Rather, their goal seems to be psychological and social manipulation. A few of the leading UFO researchers have recognized this, among them John Keel (*The Eight Tower*; *UFOs: Operation Trojan Horse*) and Jacques Vallee (*Messengers of Deception*). These researchers believe that the UFO entities are deliberately programming their human observers with false information in order to hide their true nature and purpose.

Dr. Vallee has addressed the UN on UFOs and was the model for "Lacombe" in Steven Spielberg's film "Close Encounters of the Third Kind." He has spent over two decades in serious UFO research. Like veteran UFO researcher John Keel, he has put his intellectual finger on the lowest common denominator of UFO contacts—deception—and also on the most common parallel to UFO phenomena—paganism and demonology.

He and other researchers have observed that overall and worldwide there are serious social, religious, and cultural implications to UFO phenomena because "belief in the reality of UFOs is spreading rapidly in all areas of society throughout the world."[23] Vallee puts forth the idea that UFOs are purposely hoping to "change our belief systems" and that they are engaging in a "worldwide enterprise of subliminal seduction.'"[24]

The immense popularity of books such as those by Erich von Daniken, claiming that humanity is in some sense the product of highly advanced life forms who have been guiding our evolution, reveals that people, having forsaken the concept of divine intervention, are more and more open to the concept of extraterrestrial intervention. Vallee argues that UFOs "are helping to create a new form of belief, an expectation of actual contact among large parts of the public. In turn this expectation makes millions of people hope for the imminent realization of that age-old dream: salvation from above, surrender to the greater power of some wise navigators of the cosmos...."[25]

But Vallee argues that instead, UFOs are actually placing "human beings under the control of a strange force that is bending them in absurd ways, forcing them to play a role in a bizarre game of deception.... If UFOs make an impact on our social reality, they are bound to change our political realities as well."[26]

On an individual level, thousands of individuals claim to have made contact with UFOs or their occupants. Few people can deny that society may now be poised to accept the concept of contact on a truly grand scale.

But what exactly will we be accepting?

3. Why is the Extraterrestrial Hypothesis (ETH) not credible for explaining the current UFO phenomenon?

The most popular theory by far concerning UFOs is that they represent physical craft carrying intelligent life from outer space. Unfortunately, this theory has never been credible, at least for the UFO phenomena we are experiencing.

Consider the British journal *Flying Saucer Review*, widely recognized as the leading UFO publication in the world. This periodical supports an assemblage of over 50 experts and specialists worldwide who conduct major UFO-encounter investigations. Established in 1955, it is one of the few journals that has objectively and thoroughly evaluated the phenomenon worldwide for almost 40 years. Yet an official FSR statement by editor Gordon Creighton reads, "There seems to be no evidence yet that any of these craft or beings originate from outer space."[27] Coming from a periodical of such weight, this is no trivial conclusion.

Yet it is hardly surprising. For example, Dr. Weldon's previous books listed many of the problems with the ETH including: a) Radar has never recorded the actual entering of UFOs into our atmosphere;[28] b) even with millions of advanced civilizations in outer space, it would be almost impossible if just *once* a year an extraterrestrial craft were to find us out here on the limb of our galaxy, yet we are seeing literally tens of thousands of craft yearly; c) the "aliens" seem to be able to live in our atmosphere without the help of respiratory devices; d) UFOs have been fired upon scores of times by American, Russian, and Canadian pilots, but these pilots have never been able to physically bring down a craft or capture it;[29] e) no two UFOs ever appear exactly alike, implying that other civilizations must build and use their craft only once, which would be incredible. Also militating against the ETH are the statistical considerations against life in outer space,[30] the bizarre characteristics of the UFO phenomenon itself, and the high occult correlation and strong parallel to demonic powers.

Again, the diversity and behavior of both the craft and the entities in Close Encounter episodes simply do not fit with what we would expect from advanced intergalactic travelers. If we include abduction and contactee experiences, it becomes virtually impossible to believe in the ETH. The psychology and bizarre actions of the entities more fit the demons of old, not a technically advanced and highly rational form of extraterrestrial life.[31]

Is it reasonable to think there would be no body of evidence whatever to prove that great numbers of alien physical craft are crisscrossing the skies? Is it conceivable that in the last 50 years there have been thousands (or, as some researchers have postulated, millions),[32] of different crafts circling the earth simultaneously from thousands of different places in the universe? Where is the proof?

Why should there have been an explosion of the phenomena since 1948? Why have none of these representatives of intelligent civilizations revealed themselves openly? Could thousands of civilizations from diverse points all agree as to the necessity for silence? For what purpose? And why have all of them come to the earth? In addition, if they are really extraterrestrials from outer space, why do they so closely mimic the creatures from our occult traditions on earth?

In fact, were it not for the widespread hope of human contact with extraterrestrials, the idea that UFOs represent interstellar craft would be long forgotten. We think there is only one reason why the Extraterrestrial Hypothesis is widely accepted: because so many people *want* to believe it. The evidence for it is not only lacking, but its flaws are fatal.

Even Dr. Vallee is forced to concede the tremendous researcher bias in favor of the ETH: "I also discovered that I could expect *no* cooperation from most of the UFO believers, who were willing to help me only to the extent that my conclusions would support their preconceived idea that UFOs are extraterrestrial visitors to the earth."[33] Here, and in his book *Dimensions*, Vallee proceeds to discuss many additional facts that mitigate against the ETH.[34]

Further, in light of the messages given by the UFO entities, how credible is it to think that literally thousands of genuine extraterrestrials would fly millions or billions of light years simply to teach New Age philosophy, deny Christianity, and support the occult? Why would they do this with the preponderance of such activity already occurring on this planet? And why would the entities actually possess and inhabit people just like demons do if they were really advanced extraterrestrials? Why would they consistently lie about things which we know are true, and why would they purposely deceive their contacts?

All this is why a number of UFO researchers have concluded that UFOs *are* real but do *not* necessarily originate from other planets.[35,36] For example, Brad Steiger thinks the chances are very good that "we are dealing with a multidimensional paraphysical phenomenon which is largely indigenous to planet earth."[37] Even the famous science fiction writer Arthur Clarke observes, "One theory that can no longer be taken very seriously is that UFOs are interstellar spaceships."[38]

So what are they? This brings us to our next section.

SECTION TWO

UFOs and the Occult

Evangelist Billy Graham observed, "Some Christian writers have speculated that UFOs could very well be a part of God's angelic host who preside over the physical affairs of universal creation," and he proceeds to note that even sincere Christians with a strong commitment to Scripture "contend that these UFOs are angels."[39]

Mr. Graham does not expressly cite his personal views on the subject, but he does note that "UFOs are astonishingly angel-like in some of their reported appearances."[40] This cannot be denied. But what is frequently overlooked is that the biblical demons themselves are angels—fallen angels at war with God and man. They are lying spirits who seek to deceive people spiritually.

Although the prevailing bias concerning UFO phenomena underscores an extraterrestrial hypothesis, a number of leading researchers are convinced that this is impossible. In its place they present a theory that unbiasedly examines the occult nature of the UFO phenomenon. These leading UFO researchers propose a theory asserting that 1) UFOs represent an intelligent life form, 2) they have been with man from the beginning of time, although assuming different forms throughout recorded history, 3) they do not originate from advanced civilizations in outer space but rather from another dimension or reality that coexists in the unseen world with mankind, and 4) that whatever UFOs represent, they are clearly a psychic phenomenon with the capacity to operate, at least temporarily, on the physical level. Indeed, few unbiased researchers can logically deny that UFO experiences are of an occult nature. If we catalog the basic characteristics of the occult and compare them to UFO phenomena, we discover an essential similarity.[41]

Nevertheless, these researchers have put their finger on the essentially psychic or *supernatural* quality of the UFO phenomenon.*

---

* Although some of those with a materialistic, extraterrestrial bias tend to reinterpret the supernatural nature of UFOs as the products ("supertechnology") of

Indeed, a demonic theory would predict just these things for UFOs. After 20 years of research, we believe that the demonic theory dovetails extremely well with the totality of UFO phenomena. For example, the connection to spiritism has been pointed out by B. Schwartz, C. Wilson, Clark and Coleman, B. Steiger, T. James, D. Scott Rogo, and many others.[42] In fact, we know of no UFO contactee who is not basically a spiritistic medium. In addition, we have read hundreds of articles from the oldest and most respected UFO journal, the British *Flying Saucer Review*, that indicate the psychic and/or nonextraterrestrial aspect of UFOs which, given their actions and messages, indicate probable demonic origin.

Consider just a few parallels between classical demonology and ufology. An examination of nineteenth-century literature on the occult, such as Francis Barret's authoritative work, *The Magus—Book 2* (1801), describes fallen angels or demons this way:

> ... some that are near to us wander up and down in this obscure air; others inhabit lakes, rivers and seas; others the earth and terrify earthly things ... and vex not only men but also other creatures; some being content with laughter and derision only, do contrive rather to weary men than to hurt them; some ... changing themselves into different forms, do disturb men with vain fear....[43]

A few pages later it continues, "... so demons speak; and what man does with a sensible [physical] voice, they do by impressing the conception of speech in those to whom they speak after a better manner than if they should express it in an audible voice ... yet oftentimes they send forth an audible voice."[44]

In his *Earth's Earliest Ages and Their Connection with Modern Spiritualism and Theosophy* (1876), G.H. Pember observes that the occultist "is brought into intelligent communication with the spirits of the air, and can receive any

---

an extremely scientifically advanced culture, this wishful thinking cannot explain the occult aspects of the UFO phenomenon as a whole (e.g., contactees). Further, if some kind of alien technology, whether indigenous to the planet Earth or extraterrestrial, produces phenomena that are indistinguishable from the world of the occult historically, where does one find a scorecard? How does one determine "science" from occultism? How does one determine that which is neutral from that which is demonic? To say UFOs represent a supertechnology indistinguishable from classical occultism only confuses the issue.

knowledge which they possess, or any false impression which they choose to impart . . . the demons seem permitted to do various wonders at their request."[45]

Even the great theologian Augustine once noted, "What men can do with real colors and substances the demons can very easily do by showing unreal forms. . . ."[46]

The extraterrestrial hypothesis is a prized pet theory for many people, and to question it is considered unscientific. To posit a *demonic* theory is believed a bit much, irrespective of its explanatory value. In one sense this reaction is understandable, since such a theory tends to portray UFO researchers and promoters as being somewhat in collusion with the devil. Yet having come to such a conclusion honestly, one cannot easily dismiss one's convictions. And even skeptics have had to confess that "demonology is certainly one of the logical possibilities."[47] The phenomenon certainly *appears* demonic, and therefore to parade it as exciting or benevolent encounters with highly advanced extraterrestrials would do a disservice to society. Certainly, if the phenomenon is demonic, UFO researchers should be careful about what they endorse, or even investigate.

In fact, academic integrity requires that such a theory should not be prejudged and rejected without consideration to all the facts. Again, if UFOs are demonic, to fail to identify them accurately may have far-reaching consequences at both the individual and social levels.

4. Who are some of the leading UFO researchers who recognize that UFOs are an occultic and/or demonic phenomenon?

Regrettably, most UFO researchers have not yet understood the real nature of UFOs, or the true issues surrounding them. The spiritistic theory, the most logical explanation, is rejected either because of a preexisting materialistic bias, mere skepticism, or the captivating hope of genuine contact with advanced extraterrestrial life forms.

For example, the groundbreaking work of John Keel, Dr. Jacques Vallee, and others—and its implications—has often been ignored by serious UFO researchers. Concerning his own work, Vallee complains, "The realization that none of this material has ever been seriously examined . . . is staggering. . . . What the public learns about the phenomenon comes from that small portion of the facts that has been preselected by believers to promote enthusiastic support for the extraterrestrial theory."[48]

But it should also be mentioned that a sizable number of researchers formerly committed to the extraterrestrial hypothesis have been convinced by the evidence that UFOs are of a paraphysical or occultic nature.[49] For example, Raymond Fowler, the author of five books on UFOs, confesses, "I [have] watched in dismay as a number of respected UFO researchers moved from a *physical* to a *parapsychological* interpretation of the bizarre UFO phenomenon.... Now, I [too] am being forced to reexamine the UFO phenomenon in light of its apparent paraphysical nature."[50]

No less an authority than Dr. Vallee has concluded:

> We are dealing with a yet unrecognized level of consciousness, independent of man but closely linked to the earth.... I do not believe anymore that UFOs are simply the spacecraft of some race of extraterrestrial visitors. This notion is too simplistic to explain their appearance, the frequency of their manifestations throughout recorded history, and the structure of the information exchanged with them during contact.[51]

Below we present a selected list of prominent researchers who have concluded that UFOs represent an occultic and/or demonic phenomenon.

Lynn E. Catoe. In 1969 the U.S. Government Printing Office issued a publication researched by the Library of Congress for the U.S. Air Force Office of Scientific Research: *UFOs and Related Subjects: An Annotated Bibliography.* Listing over 1600 books and articles, it was the most comprehensive bibliography of the period. The senior bibliographer was Lynn Catoe; her literature survey required two full years to read through thousands of books, articles, and publications in order to prepare the volume of over 400 pages. In her preface she observes the following:

> A large part of the available UFO literature is closely linked with mysticism and the metaphysical. It deals with subjects like mental telepathy, automatic writing and invisible entities as well as phenomena like poltergeist [ghost] manifestations and "possession." Many of the UFO reports now being published in the popular press recount alleged incidents that are strikingly similar to demonic possession and psychic phenomena....[52]

Dr. Pierre Guerin. Dr. Guerin is an eminent scientist associated with the French National Council for Scientific Research. After examining and discrediting all reasonable hope for the extraterrestrial hypothesis and rejecting as implausible the solely human (e.g., psychological) theories, he concludes that UFO "behavior is more akin to magic than to physics as we know it."[53] He then emphasizes that "the modern UFOnauts and the demons of past days are probably identical."[54] Although it is rare to find a scientist and UFO expert of Guerin's stature who is willing to admit that the demonological connection does have relevance to UFO data, his materialistic bias emerges when he concludes that the supernatural manifestations of the UFOs are a consequence of their own "supertechnology."[55] Nevertheless, even Guerin believes, "What is quite certain is that the phenomenon is active here on our planet, and active here as *master*."[56]

John A. Keel. John Keel is considered by some to be among the most informed persons in the world on UFOs. He has spent decades doing firsthand research among people who have had all kinds of UFO encounters, but especially among those who have had close contacts. He knows the field as well as anyone and has written numerous books on the subject, including the now-classic *UFOs: Operation Trojan Horse* as well as *The Mothman Prophecies*, *The Eighth Tower*, and *Our Haunted Planet*. These and other of his books are a gold mine of documentation revealing the occult/demonic nature of the UFO phenomena. After surveying the literature of demonology, he observes, "The manifestations and occurrences described in this imposing literature are similar if not entirely identical to the UFO phenomenon itself."[57] We may summarize Keel's research with this statement by him: "The UFO manifestations seem to be, by and large, merely minor variations of the age-old demonological phenomenon."[58] This is why other veteran UFO researchers like Trevor James observe, "A working knowledge of occult science . . . is indispensable to UFO investigation."[59] In the words of sociologists Stupple and McNeece, "studies of flying saucer cults repeatedly show that they are part of a larger occult social world."[60]

Jacques Vallee. Dr. Vallee is also considered by many to be among the world's leading investigators of UFO phenomena and is the author of eight books on the subject. In his third book, *Passport to Magonia*, he describes 923 UFO landings from 1868-1968. Again and again we discover references to a wide variety of occult phenomena while the demonic nature of UFOs is evident throughout. In *Messengers of Deception* he observes that an "impressive parallel [can] be made between UFO occupants and the popular conception of demons"[61] and that UFOs can "project images or fabricated scenes designed to change our belief systems."[62] In *The Invisible College* he argues that the source of power behind UFOs constitutes a powerful worldwide force that has been influential in shaping human beliefs throughout history: "human belief...is being controlled and conditioned," "man's concepts are being rearranged," and we may be headed toward "a massive change of human attitudes toward paranormal abilities and extraterrestrial life."[63]

In *Confrontations* he points out:

> The "medical examination" to which abductees are said to be subjected, often accompanied by sadistic sexual manipulation, is reminiscent of the medieval tales of encounters with demons. It makes no sense in a sophisticated or technical or biological framework: any intelligent being equipped with the scientific marvels that UFOs possess would be in a position to achieve any of these alleged scientific objectives in a shorter time and with fewer risks.[64]

Citing the extensive research of Bertrand Meheust [*Science-Fiction et Soucoupes Volantes* (Paris, 1978); *Soucoupes Volantes et Folklore* (Paris, 1985)], Vallee also reveals that "the symbolic display seen by the abductees is identical to the type of initiation ritual or astral voyage that is imbedded in the [occult] traditions of every culture."[65] Thus, "The structure of abduction stories is identical to that of occult initiation rituals."[66] And, "The UFO beings of today belong to the same class of manifestation as the [occult] entities that were described in centuries past...."[67] He elsewhere observes that in terms of their profound effect on us, we are seemingly helpless to prevent it, so that in the end, "it doesn't matter where they come from."[68]

Ivar Mackay. E.A.I. Mackay was a former chairman of the respected British UFO Research Association and spent half a lifetime researching the field of the occult and parapsychology. In examining the entities found in the occult with those found among UFO phenomena, he observes their parallel nature:

> Further, if one sets the three occult groups against the three classifications of UFO entities and their characteristics, it is rather surprising how complementary to each other they appear to be, not only through their appearance, activities, and level of behavior, but also in the quality of mental and, especially, emotional reaction and response that has been noted to have occurred on contact.[69]

His two-part research article, "UFOs and the Occult," describes a large number of similarities between UFOs and occult phenomena and yet is drawn largely from *noncontactee* UFO encounters; many of the correlations are found in the literature of mediumism and seance manifestations.[70]

Kenneth Ring and Others. UFO experiences parallel many occult experiences, such as astral travel and even its cousin, the "Near-Death Experience" (NDE). In our *Facts on Life After Death*, we have documented the characteristically occult nature of the NDE.

In *Journal of UFO Studies*, Vol. 2, 1990, near-death-experience researchers Kenneth Ring and Christopher J. Rosing of the Department of Psychology, University of Connecticut, suggest that UFO experiences (UFOE) and near-death experiences (NDE) are in many ways "functionally equivalent."[71] For example, they report that individuals who experience encounters with UFOs or NDEs as adults had frequently become sensitive to occult realities as children.[72] They also observe, "There are wide-ranging and powerful, psychophysical changes following either a UFOE or NDE."[73] Among the common items experienced in both categories are an increase in energy currents in the body, mind expansion, information flooding, and psychic abilities.[74] They conclude that, apparently, "psycho-physical changes reported in connection with UFOEs and NDEs reflect some sort of psychobiological transformation," and they propose occultic *kundalini* energy as a possible or probable explanation. Thus, "Kundalini activation is much more likely...to be reported afterward by experiential respondents than controls, and, as before, this is equally true for NDErs and UFOErs alike."[75]

Participants in both UFO and NDE encounters agree that these encounters involve an integral part of a dramatic New Age evolutionary transformation now emerging among humanity: "...these experiences reflect a purposive intelligence...they are part of an accelerating evolutionary current that is propelling the human race toward higher [occult] consciousness and heightened spirituality."[76]

These authors conclude with the following:

> What repeatedly struck us most forcibly was the undeniable overall *similarity* between our two experiential groups, UFOErs and NDErs.... We should now consider that despite the differences in the nature of these experiences, they may have a common underlying source—whatever that source may be.[77]

No one can deny that even many non-Christian researchers have concluded that the UFO phenomenon is an occult one. If it can be established that the world of the occult is the masterpiece of the biblical Satan and his demons, then it is logical to conclude that UFOs constitute a demonic phenomenon with a hidden agenda.*

5. What powerful illustration can be given to reveal the demonic nature of the UFO phenomenon?

A booklet this size does not permit citing a large variety of illustrations from actual UFO encounters documenting the demonic nature of these contacts, but the number of such encounters is vast.[78]

However, bestselling novelist Whitley Strieber is a good example of the demonic reality that is so easily encountered through UFO experiences. Reading about his personal UFO encounters can be terrifying. Strieber, who has a strong background in the occult (Zen, tarot cards, altered states of consciousness, Gurdjieff and Ouspenjsky),[79] is the author of a number of award-winning or bestselling books which frequently deal with the realm of the occult (*The Hunger*, *Black Magic*, *Night Church*, *Cat Magic*, and *The Wolfen*). His two UFO books have also been bestsellers: *Communion*, which was on the *New York Times* bestseller list for eight months, and its sequel, *Transformation*.

The UFO entities that Strieber has contacted are evil, and Strieber has sensed this. But UFO contacts usually seem to be manipulated into accepting that the entities are "benevolent" in spite of two sobering facts: 1) contrary *data* which reveal that the entities are other than what they claim, and 2) an initial *sensing* of evil. These entities are clever enough to make Strieber think they care about him. Yet his torment by them never ceases. Whatever his relationship to the entities, and he increasingly concludes that their involvement with him is something "good," he also remains terrified of them and uncertain as to what they are.

Thus the severe mental and spiritual disruptions that characteristically frequent those who have experiences with UFO entities are all too common in Mr. Strieber's account. Therefore a brief mention is relevant. Characteristically, these UFO experiences include the following: The occult background of the subject; the dramatic manipulation of mental experiences; poltergeist events; the ever-present experience of supposedly "missing" time; mental

---

* In *Cult Watch* we have documented that Satan and his demons are the power behind the world of the occult.

terrorism; profound and drastic personality changes; social notoriety and/or stigma; dramatic continuing aftereffects and contacts with the entities; an initial intuitive sense of tremendous fear and frequently evil; and numerous correlations to ancient paganism which "haunt" the relationship.

Below we cite a few of Mr. Strieber's firsthand experiences with his allegedly "benign" UFO contacts:

> I became entirely given over to extreme dread. The fear was so powerful that it seemed to make my personality completely evaporate.... "Whitley" ceased to exist. What was left was a body and a state of raw fear so great that it swept about me like a thick, suffocating curtain, turning paralysis into a condition that seemed close to death.... I died, and a wild animal appeared in my place.[80]

Although frequently confessing that he also was *treated* like a wild animal, he realized that the entities were attempting to profoundly transform his very being. He recalls, "I had been captured like a wild animal on December 26 [and] rendered helpless.... They had changed me, done something to me. I could sense it clearly that night but I could not articulate it.... I wondered if there was any relationship between my experience and the mystic walk of the shaman, or the night ride of the witch."[81]

Later his growing fears caused him to doubt his own sanity. "I was doubly worried now for my sanity.... The visitors persisted in my mind like glowing coals.... Whatever this was, it had been involved with me for years. I really squirmed."[82]

Strieber's recollection of his encounters with the aliens is reminiscent of other demonic visits, including the smell of sulfur. For example, "I had an awful feeling. I felt their presence. It was palpable. Most upsetting, I could smell them."[83] He describes one of the aliens as "what seemed almost to be a demon with a narrow face and dark, slanted eyes. It spoke to me in a high, squeaky voice."[84]

In *Transformation*, the sequel to *Communion*, Strieber continues to wonder about both the nature and the motives of the UFO entities:

> Why were my visitors so secretive, hiding themselves behind my consciousness? I could only conclude that they were using me and did not want me to know why. ... What if they were dangerous? Then I was terribly dangerous because I was playing a role in acclimatizing people to them.[85]

Eventually he realized he was embroiled in a battle that might claim much more than his physical existence:

> Increasingly I felt as if I were entering a struggle that might even be more than life-or-death. It might be a struggle for my soul, my essence, or whatever part of me might have reference to the eternal. There are worse things than death, I suspected.... So far the word *demon* had never been spoken among the scientists and doctors who were working with me.... Alone at night I worried about the legendary cunning of demons.... At the very least, I was going stark, raving mad.[86]

Strieber became tormented: "I could not dispel my fear. I'd already determined that not one human soul knows a single certain thing about the visitors. Nobody."[87] He also realized that the entities could not be trusted. "I couldn't get any reassurance from the visitors. I couldn't get even the breath of a promise—let alone a guarantee—that they wouldn't hurt me."[88] But hurt him they did, time and time again, brutally and sadistically. Is it surprising that he recalls other sensings of the demonic? "I wondered if I might not be in the grip of demons, if they were not making me suffer for their own purposes, or simply for their enjoyment."[89]

> I felt an absolutely indescribable sense of menace. It was hell on earth to be there [in the presence of the entities], and yet I couldn't move, couldn't cry out, couldn't get away. I'd lay as still as death, suffering inner agonies. Whatever was there seemed so monstrously ugly, so filthy and dark and sinister. Of course they were demons. They had to be. And they were here and I couldn't get away....[90]

Strieber was hooked, but he had no means of escape. "My mind was thick with the visitors. They were so terrible, so ugly, so fierce, and I was so small and helpless. I could smell that odor of theirs like greasy smoke hanging in my nostrils."[91]

Unfortunately, demons have an insidious capacity to draw and attract their contacts in sinister ways no matter how appalling their torments. And so Strieber became their victim. Convinced that their torture of him was for his own ultimate "good," he confesses, "Again, though, I felt love. Despite all the ugliness and the terrible things that had been done [to me], I found myself longing for them, missing them! How was this possible?"[92]

The fear and terror experienced by Strieber are not surprising. He was not only thrust into an alien world; it was a world in which he had lost control—indeed, he had become one controlled.

All this raises an important question: Why should things like this be experienced from advanced extraterrestrials if they are really beings who have evolved into an enlightened society and now spend their time exploring the universe in perfect benevolence? Doesn't it make more sense that if we can sometimes sense *evil* in other humans we may also sense *evil* in malevolent spirits? Despite his attraction to and love for the entities, why does he describe them as "looking *mean*," as having "the souls of pirates," and as having an "intense hatred" for him? Why does he still wonder, "Is this the devil?"[93] Why the constant perception of fear, terror, and distrust, as well as a sensing of the demonic, if these are really benevolent beings from outer space?

Strieber himself has contacted many other people who have had similar hellish experiences. "I have never before encountered such a group of seemingly ordinary people under so much pressure. They were deeply troubled by the question of what their experiences really mean. Those who have had the experience must learn to ride a sort of psychological razor."[94]

There are thousands of such people, and they too have sensed something evil and demonic. Even years after such an experience it continues to haunt and influence these people in harmful ways; they have become brutalized. They have been mentally (and sometimes physically) raped at the impersonal whim of alien forces. Never again in their lives do they feel security. They fear that at any time they may be manipulated at will by forces beyond their control.

The possibility of insanity or suicide stemming from such harrowing and tremendously dominating experiences should not be neglected. Not everyone can successfully integrate the kinds of horrors that UFO experiences may bring. Strieber himself confesses that the experience of contact is so stressful that people who are unable to integrate it "are often shattered."[95]

As in shamanism and other virulent forms of the occult, the encounter often produces one of two things: more frequently 1) integration and occult transformation, but sometimes 2) insanity or death. Strieber further observes, "I wish that I could believe that the experience had never

urt anybody. But I couldn't believe that, not in view of the
errific stress I had been under.... It was intolerable. The
ay before I met Budd Hopkins [a UFO investigator] I
lmost jumped out a window."[96]

Stuart Goldman, a newspaper writer, has talked with
Vhitley Strieber on several occasions and investigated
JFOs as a skeptical reporter. After describing Strieber's
ncounters with UFO entities, which he refers to as "his
ormenters," he provides the following discussion:[97]

> But the real question remains. Who *are* these beings
> that apparently enjoy inflicting untold amounts of
> pain on innocent victims? Elaine Morganelli, one of
> the guests at Strieber's LA meeting, came up with
> the simple, yet chilling answer. Morganelli's conclu-
> sion is that Strieber is being contacted not by friendly
> visitors, but by demons....

> "People can be duped by devils," Morganelli says. "A
> [demonic] spirit can tell you anything. They love to
> fool you. These people [the UFO abductees] are being
> taken over. The more you go along with it, the harder
> it is to get away from it."

> But to what purpose? "I think they're being used to
> get an anti-Christian movement going," Morganelli
> said of the abductees. "What got me was when he
> [Whitley] referred to the Lord and his angels as
> 'Nazis of the air.' When he said that I thought, 'Oh
> boy, that's it. I'm out of here.'"

Goldman comments:

> One could write Morganelli off as some sort of Chris-
> tian fanatic. However, she's not the only one who's
> come to the conclusion that Strieber's visitors—and in
> turn the beings who are abducting countless thousands
> of people—are nothing more than good old-fashion
> demons, doing what they do best: stealing souls.

After citing a number of examples of researchers who
aave concluded that the UFO phenomenon is evil or demonic,
Goldman offers the observations of the late authority on
ults and the occult, Dr. Walter Martin, who told him, "The
ig problem is not *what* they are but *who* they are." Martin
writes, "The key to it is their theology. They're all saying
he same thing, and all of it is bad-mouthing the Bible. This
ells me that what the Bible says was going to take place *is*

taking place. What you're dealing with is another dimension of reality which the Bible frequently mentions. It's called 'the realm of the prince of the powers of the air.' In other words, this is a supernatural manifestation which Christianity, Islam, and Judaism would all call demonic."

"Look," Martin says, "I don't think that there's a devil behind every bush and tree. I'm just saying, what would we expect at the end of the ages in our advanced culture? We would expect a manifestation that would fit into our time frame. What better way to attract us than with intergalactic visitors? . . . We're *obsessed* with them!"[98]

Stuart Goldman, himself a hard-nosed reporter, concludes his research with the following comments:

> . . . the unpleasant fact is, fifty thousand people cannot be lying. *Something* is here—probing people, inspecting them, and planting thoughts in their minds, manipulating their bodies—treating them, in a sense, like so many cattle. Is it all simply a gigantic cosmic joke, or is there a more sinister plot at hand? Are we seeing the formation of a new and highly destructive cult, one whose view posits the elimination (the New Agers call it "spiritual cleansing") of people who are "unfit" to exist in the coming New World? . . . Are there *really* demonic entities hovering about, searching for likely candidates whose brains and minds they can invade, filling them full of fairytales and lies—fattening them for the kill?
>
> The answer is not easily forthcoming. But whichever scenario you may choose, the ominous statement of John Keel must—for all but the most hardened skeptics—ring in our ears.
>
> "The earth is not inhabited," says Keel. "It's infested."[99]

In conclusion, one cannot adequately convey the terror and tragedy that frequently stalks those who have a deep experience with UFO beings.

The phenomenon is clearly demonic. In our library and files we have over a thousand cases of UFO contact that can only be described in this manner. Interested readers may consult hundreds of examples in the documented literature such as the British *Flying Saucer Review*. As veteran UFO researcher Janet Gregory notes, ". . . the features listed above as pertaining to demons crop up again and again in UFO reports."[100] This is also why noted UFO researcher Jonathan Caplan observes that "a strong body of opinion [now

xists] to campaign for the terms of reference for the UFO
investigation to include such subjects as occult religion,
parapsychology, spiritualism, folklore, and demonology."[101]

. How do those who claim to be in close contact with UFOs and UFO entities illustrate the occultic nature of UFO phenomena?

If the UFO phenomena were actually extraterrestrial, it
seems a bit odd that the advanced beings associated with
them would act in their communications in the same manner that demons do with their human hosts—as in seance
mediumism, channeling, and other forms of spiritism. Many
researchers have noted the striking parallels between methods of UFO contact and those characteristically found in the
world of the occult. In their *The Unidentified*, researchers
Clark and Coleman observe that modern UFO contactees
and mediums are one and the same: "In the considerable
majority of cases the contact experience, which comprises
the core of the enigma, occurs in a state of altered consciousness.... We see no alternative but to view the flying saucer
contactee as a modern day spiritualist medium, religious
mystic, shaman...etc."[102]

The experienced psychical researcher and college pro-
fessor Brad Steiger also notes that while in communication
with the alleged extraterrestrials most contactees are nearly
indistinguishable from mediums at a seance.[103] This is
why Trevor James observes that some contactees establish
communication with the UFO entities "after preparatory
measures closely resembling those of a seance...."[104]

Bryant and Helen Reeve spent two years and traveled
over 23,000 miles interviewing and living with UFO contactees. In their *Flying Saucer Pilgrimage* they observe
that contact between people and the UFO entities is characteristically through occult means. For example, they list
automatic writing, telepathy, mediumship, Eastern medi-
tation, psychic materializations, the so-called "Akashic"
records, and many more.[105]

Religion authority Dr. Robert S. Ellwood of the University of Southern California observes that for both UFO
contactees and spiritualist mediums:

> Both types of groups employ the same manner of
> communication: vision and marvelous journeys, trance
> speaking and writing, seance circles, and telepathy.
> The close interaction between Spiritualism and UFO
> cults is not surprising, for one finds there is much

exchange of persons between them....In some cases individual contactees have delivered trance message from UFOs in a manner virtually identical to th trance-preaching of Spiritualism.[106]

Elsewhere he correctly points out concerning contactees "Their practices and forms of expression seem mostly derived from Spiritualism, with the principal contactee playin the role of a major medium."[107]

Again, the reason these connections between UFO phe nomena and mediumism are so natural is because the UF(phenomenon is simply a more cleverly packaged form c mediumistic phenomena. For example, if we examine psy choanalyst and psychical researcher Dr. Nandor Fodor' *Encyclopedia of Psychic Science*, we find it to be a wealth c information not only on the world of the occult, principall; mediumism and spiritism, but also on UFO phenomena Again and again, in hundreds of cases, the phenomena h cites from seance mediumism and the occult are right out c modern ufology.[108] Not surprisingly, the late leading psy chical researcher D. Scott Rogo correctly observed that "th history of mediumship is littered with accounts of sucl [UFO] contact."[109]

Poltergeists are a hallmark of occult phenomena and ar also frequently associated with UFOs. There is a strikin, parallel between UFO "flaps" (large numbers of sighting in a relatively short period of time) and poltergeist out breaks both numerically and geographically.[110] Dr. Valle observes, "It is the rule, rather than the exception, to fin significant UFO sightings preceded or followed by othe anomalies, notably of the poltergeist variety."[111]

In both the world of UFOs and occultism, contactee experience a radical change in their lives that almost alway involves a drastic change in both personality and worldviev which are now complementary to occultism. Sometime these radical transformations occur from nothing mor than witnesses being caught in a beam of light from th UFO.[112]

Perhaps there is no more striking hallmark of the occul than that of spirit possession. There are literally thousand of documented cases, many involving very ugly endings.[11] But this phenomenon is similar if not identical to the pos session of UFO contactees, as well as some Close Encounte UFO cases. Whether in the occult or ufology, the person i taken over by the invading entity, sometimes voluntaril; sometimes involuntarily, and controlled by the creature fo whatever purposes it has in mind.

Among UFO contactees or others who communicate personally with the alleged extraterrestrials there are also literally thousands of cases of what can only be termed spirit possession. Incidents of possession are mentioned by Keel, Steiger, Norman, Catoe, Vallee, Schwartz, Reeve, and a dozen others.[114] Indeed, a large number of famous UFO contactees had an occult or mediumistic background even prior to contact: Adamski, Van Tassle, Menger, etc., all the way up to the modern Whitley Strieber.[115] In fact, we have personally talked with a number of alleged abductees and/or contactees who have clearly been demon-possessed. And many spirit-possessed mediums who are not even seeking UFO communication may end up being contacted and becoming channels for both "the dead" and "extraterrestrials."[116] The fact that these supposedly advanced beings from outer space prefer to possess their contacts after the manner of demons is further evidence that we are dealing with an occult phenomenon.

7. Are the "special messages" that the alleged extraterrestrials claim they are giving to mankind the same as those found in the world of the occult?

If we were really being contacted by highly advanced extraterrestrial civilizations, one might expect some evidence for it in the thousands of messages that have been dutifully recorded by their human contacts. Unfortunately, these messages do not reflect a highly advanced scientific culture. Rather, they reflect the decadence of ancient paganism and the occult. In fact, the messages of the alleged extraterrestrials, beginning in the early 1950s, is little different from the message of modern New Age religion. One could even argue that it was the UFO contactees who really began the modern New Age movement, and not the pundits of the 1970s.[117] Nevertheless, we have examined scores of such messages, and, as many researchers have noted, none can deny that they offer us the same old occultism. Brad Steiger, who has investigated hundreds of cases, confesses that "whether men and women claim to be in contact with Space Brothers, Ascended Masters, or spirits from the astral plane, they are all independently coming up with largely the same communications."[118]

E.A.I. Mackay observes, "It is an interesting fact that the information gained due to human involvement with extraspacial entities in the field of ufology is almost exactly mirrored by what has been understood within the Esoteric [i.e., occult] fraternities from time immemorial."[119]

No less an authority than John Keel observes that "the endless messages from the space people would now fill a library, and while the communicators claim to represent some other world, the contents of those messages are identical to the messages long received by mediums and mystics."[120]

So what are the messages from these advanced extraterrestrials deep in space? According to scores of books by contactees that we have read, they teach 1) that biblical religion is false and outdated; 2) that man must develop his psychic ability; 3) that we are at the threshold of a New Age of occult enlightenment; 4) that God and man or the creation are part of the same divine essence (pantheism) and 5) that extradimensional entities are now present to assist mankind in leaving the "old ways" and adjusting to the New Age of spiritual advancement. Nor should we neglect the recurring theme that some forms of drastic authoritarian social control may be necessary to assure the survival of this planet.[121]

8. UFO entities: What other evidence would lead a person to conclude that UFO beings are not extraterrestrials but are part of the world of the occult?

Around the globe there are tens of thousands of reported "UFO entity" cases, thousands involving human abduction reports. These entities range in size from just a few inches to almost 20 feet, but usually between four and seven feet. They appear in forms that are human or humanoid, robot or animal-like, bizarre or ghostly. Sometimes these entities exhibit deliberate hostility toward humans which has resulted in physical or psychological harm, and even possession by the entity. Most of the time they feign an aloofness toward man, or in contactee cases a genuine "concern." Sometimes, just like UFOs, these beings appear independently in three-dimensional space and time, while at other times they exist only in the experience of the "observer."

The morphology (form) of the UFO "occupants" suggests ties to the earth—not outer space. Classification of the entities corresponds broadly to creatures of historic folklore, mythology, demonology and occultism in a wide variety of times and cultures. The fact that the UFO entities fit historic patterns of previously existing morphological types from many occultic traditions argues for their being indigenous to this planet. Both Lawson and Vallee have done interesting and important work in this field.[122] It is significant that Lawson himself observes that the devil "is a polymorph and so can mimic any form imaginable, or change his size at will."[123]

Whatever the UFO entities are, they are not physical beings from material worlds deep in space. Let us cite an illustration of why we believe this. If one examines parapsychologist and former president of the Society for Psychical Research George N.M. Tyrrell's noted text *Apparitions*, one encounters an amazing description of the characteristics of UFO entities themselves, even though this book deals with the entities, poltergeists, and ghostly apparitions from the world of the occult. Again and again his description fits the experiences of those who contact the beings associated with UFOs. Tyrrell suggests that there are several important characteristics associated with occult apparitions. These are: 1) There are different ways in which apparitions can externalize themselves in space; 2) apparitions have no actual physical basis; 3) apparitions will deliberately imitate normal perception, even though they are not obligated to do so; 4) apparitions include all kinds of additional features besides the central figure, and the additions and the central figure all come into existence in the same way; 5) apparitions, whether they are visual or auditory, can sometimes be collective (experienced by many people); 6) sometimes there are cold feelings accompanying apparitions; and 7) subjective feelings of other types sometimes accompany apparitions.[124]

Tyrrell observes that one of the characteristics of apparitions is their remarkable imitation of normal perception. As far as it can, an apparition appears to aim at behaving "exactly as a living human being would behave under the attendant circumstances." It behaves as if aware of its surroundings, it stands out in space, it appears real and solid, and it is as "clear and vivid in matters of detail, such as the color and texture and clothing" as a real material person.[125]

Further, although nothing is physically present in space, something is visibly present in physical space as a visual solid: "Apparitions, then, combine two qualities. They are: a) nonphysical in character, yet, when at their best, they are b) indistinguishable from material figures normally perceived, so far as the visual and auditory senses are concerned . . . it is not uncommon for the sense of touch to be hallucinated in apparitional cases."[126]

Tyrrell also discusses apparitions that include not only multiple objects but even entire environmental settings. He comments:

> In whatever sense the central figure is "there," the auxiliary objects, the additional figures, and the environment are "there," too. . . . Apparitional dramas

need no more be confined to the portrayal of a single human figure than need a cinematographic film. The situation is rather a strange one because, although nothing is *physically* present in space, something (a *visual* solid) is *visibly* present in physical space.[127]

Nevertheless, although he concedes that the "nonphysical character of [the] apparitions is overwhelming," he also confesses that for all he knows there may be "physical apparitions as well."[128]

As noted, the features of apparitions mentioned by Tyrrell and others are striking when compared to those found in the UFO phenomenon. UFOs exhibit all these characteristics, down to the feelings of cold, and they may also be temporarily physically present.

Significantly, Tyrrell observes that whoever originates the apparitions "has the power at the same time to control normally produced sense-data as well. . . . This implies minute and accurate coordination between normal and hallucinatory sense-data. . . . There must, therefore, be psychological control of normal perception interfering at some point in what is usually supposed to be a complete psycho-physical causal sequence."[129] In other words, they influence the mind and its perceptions, including all sense perceptions. They have the capacity to produce a complete visual setting and they do so to produce experiences that can be terrifying.

As we consider the characteristics put forward by Tyrrell, it becomes clear that in the world of the occult we are considering something more than merely subjective experiences. Entire apparitional dramas can be physically present in space, observable by anyone present, and yet visually indistinguishable from reality. Further, the same experience can be mentally implanted in the mind so that only the observer "sees" it. Yet it too is indistinguishable from reality. This is exactly what we find in the world of UFOs.

9. How can one tell if a given UFO experience is real or only in the mind?

Like certain occult experiences, UFO events can be real in that they involve actual supernatural phenomena that temporarily exist in time and space. Demons who produce visual aerial phenomena or materialize as UFO entities are examples. But it is also true that other UFO experiences, such as abductions, exist only in the "observer's" mind. (Because we believe that extraterrestrial craft do not actually exist, we believe it is physically impossible for anyone to be taken on board them.)

Nevertheless, determining which UFO experience is real and which is only mentally induced can be difficult in any UFO (or occult) category. Why? Because there are many cases where, although several persons are present, only the "contactee" can actually see the phenomena. Thus, discerning the exact nature of any *individual* experience with UFOs becomes a dilemma.

Martin Luther once declared that "Satan is well able to affect all the sense so that a man would swear he did see, hear, sense, and touch a thing which notwithstanding he did not see, etc."[130]

As noted, the literature of the occult and modern ufology clearly indicates that whatever is behind the UFO phenomena, it has the ability to dramatically manipulate and influence the sense perceptions and experiences of those it contacts. For example, as a result of his experiences with UFO beings, noted scientist Andrija Puharich concluded that he "could never again know which of my experiences were directly imposed on me... and which were not. I have never been more deeply shaken in my life as when I realized the full implication of this power...."[131] We could cite scores of other examples from the literature of the occult.[132]

To understand how a UFO experience can be perceived as real, and yet isn't, consider UFO abductions. Despite literally thousands of alleged abductions, not a particle of proof has ever been produced to substantiate the claim that people were taken on board a genuine extraterrestrial craft. Hypnotic regression supplies the sole "evidence" that such an event ever occurred.[133] Indeed, hypnosis "has become a fanatical obsession with American UFO researchers today."[134]

Nevertheless, an abundance of data can be produced, some of it from UFO researchers themselves, to show that the use of hypnosis proves absolutely nothing in terms of substantiating an alleged UFO abduction.[135,136]

Significantly, "a group of subjects who knew nothing about UFOs were hypnotized and given imaginary UFO abductions. Their narratives turned out to be very similar to 'real' abductees' experiences. The entities they sketched were similar also...."[137] Further, "An average comparison of the imaginary sessions with the 'real' regressions from the literature indicated almost no substantive difference."[138]

In addition, lie detectors tests cannot prove that UFO abductees are telling the truth either, since it has been demonstrated that the effectiveness of these devices is 'practically nil, as a long list of scientific references would show."[139]

Thus UFO investigators may use all kinds of psychological testing methods from hypnosis and lie detectors to psychological tests (such as the CPI, MMPI, and PSE), and yet the best one may conclude is that a psychologically healthy person is telling the truth when he says he "knows" he experienced such and such. Of course, this does not demand that such an experience ever really occurred. John Rimmer concludes in his *Evidence for Alien Abductions* that such experiences are "almost completely psychological in origin."[140]

Because UFO abductions have no physical reality and yet are experienced, such events are better explained as episodes akin to the reality of a hypnotic episode, but having more power.

Although a human hypnotist can produce UFO abduction experiences almost identical to those who have "real" abduction experiences, there is nevertheless an additional element in the latter category. Druffel observes, "The difference is that in the actual abduction incidents there seems to be an alien [i.e., additional] stimuli interacting with the witnesses' minds."[141]

At this point the question becomes, Who then is doing the hypnotizing? Whoever controls the episode is more proficient than a human hypnotist. Indeed, the literature about demon influence and possession suggests that demons can do far more with the human organism (mind and body) than mere men are capable of. People forget that demons are not the mischievous but harmless little creatures they are usually portrayed to be; instead, they are a highly powerful form of life existing on a different level of reality—the spiritual. They are morally corrupted personal, supernatural beings at enmity with man.

Someone or something definitely wants us to believe in them. The question is, Why? We can only conclude that UFO abductions are part of the plan to fascinate humanity with exterrestrial life and all it implies. What could produce a more powerful conviction of UFO reality than actually being taken *inside* a craft, being examined, having conversations with the captain or crew, etc.? To have such an experience gives the UFO phenomenon a dimension of reality and conviction to both recipient and investigator that a CEI or II alone simply cannot supply.

In conclusion, whatever the level of reality for any given UFO experience (physical manifestation or mental implant), the overall effect is the same.

10. Why would demons want to impersonate alien beings from other worlds?

Let us begin by asking another question: Why would demons want to impersonate the human dead? Many former mediums have noted that the spirits they contacted routinely impersonated the dead.[142] The answer for this ruse is *deception*. People are fearful of death and judgment and are more than willing to listen to alleged postmortem spirits who will soothe their fears and promise them that life after death is other than what the Bible teaches. But while spirits may play on the fears of people in one instance, they may play on the hopes of people in another. Mankind has always been fascinated with the heavens (e.g., astrology), and even more so with the recent advent of the space age.

Millions of people are longing for contact with a vastly superior civilization from space in the hope that it may solve the world's problems and end war, poverty, and everything else that no one likes. This longing includes some of our leading politicians and statesmen. So it is not surprising that demons, whose primary purpose is spiritual deception (leading people away from God), would take advantage of this hope and seek to pervert it. Consider the following.

One of the most dominant cultural influences of UFOs is to undermine faith in the Bible. UFO phenomena support the myth of naturalistic evolution and the idea that man can finally perfect himself apart from God. For many people, belief in UFOs has become a replacement for personal faith in God, since the UFO entities encourage people to look to the skies (or the aliens) for their individual and collective salvation. UFO encounters also promote occultism and expand its territory under a novel and unexpected guise.

For other people, the UFO phenomenon makes the Bible anachronistic and undermines its authority by relegating it to a level of vastly more primitive, "earthbound" literature. The UFO phenomena tend to belittle mankind's place in the universe from its biblical heights to something lower. Man is no longer the crown of God's creation and the one for whom Christ died. Instead, he is something of an almost infinitely lesser creature—one lower species among probable billions of more advanced species in the universe.

Thus many extraterrestrial theorists place man as an infinitely small speck in an infinitely vast universe whose only genuine hope for survival is contacting a much more evolved form of life. But the end result is to cheapen the value of man, his being made in the image of God, and the significance of the fact that God Himself became man in the incarnation. This also tends to cheapen the concept of the atonement and Christian redemption in ways that are too complex to discuss here.

Finally, a frequent claim of the UFO contactees is that in order for mankind to progress spiritually, certain "undesirable" elements will have to be supernaturally removed from the earth: The extraterrestrials will take care of this "cleansing" of the earth, but it will require the instantaneous disappearance of millions of people. Perhaps this could become a false explanation for the rapture of the Church. Thus UFOs may play a part in the distortion of biblical eschatology. If the premillennial, pretribulational view is correct, then in the years preceding the second coming of Christ we may expect certain things such as the rapture of the Church and a one-world government.[143]

Obviously, the perceived threat of attack by a vastly superior extraterrestrial life form could be the means to unite the world in a way that would be otherwise unimaginable. Indeed, the UFO phenomenon has already caused a number of leading newspaper editorials (such as the Los Angeles Times) to speculate on just this possibility.[144]

Dr. Vallee observes the same effect in another context:

> Increased attention given to UFO activity promotes the concept of political unification of this planet. This is perhaps the most commonly recurring theme in my entire study of these groups. Through the belief in UFOs, a tremendous yearning for global peace is expressing itself. . . . Contactee philosophies often include belief in higher races and in totalitarian systems that would eliminate democracy.[145]

All the above, and more, are reasons why demons would logically seek to imitate alien life from other worlds.

11. Can we explain how UFOs are produced?

No. But from all we can deduce about the behavior of both UFOs and the entities that accompany them, it seems evident that these phenomena are produced in the same manner that other occult phenomena are produced. They involve dramatic manipulations of matter and energy. Although they originate from the spiritual world, they can produce very powerful, temporarily physical manifestations at the material level.

For example, a recent UFO sighting at the Woodbridge Air Base in England (where no less than 15 trained military personnel saw UFOs for hours on end) is characteristic.

They display intelligence. They "play" and "toy" with the observers. They send down beams of light within two feet of an observer. Animals react strongly in their presence. They leave landing indentations, tree limbs may be broken, and surrounding environmental objects may glow after the encounter. Human time and perception may be dramatically distorted, even during a CEI. Car radios and engines, as well as electronic military weapons, may cease to work. Such UFOs can be seen and tracked on radar and photographed at a distance.[146] In other cases jets sent in pursuit have sometimes disappeared; on the ground people have been injured and even killed.[147]

UFOs may instantaneously break into multiple separate objects and then simply vanish. They range in size from a few feet to literally miles in diameter, they come in all colors and shapes, and they can change their size and shape at will.[148] One encounter documented by the Soviet Academy of Sciences reported a UFO that changed "from a star-shape, to a cone, to a double-cone, to a cloud, to a plumshape, to a square, and then to a giant needle-nosed wingless aircraft."[149] UFOs may pass right through physical objects or a group of UFOs may merge into one.[150] They can perform right-angle turns and instantaneous stops at thousands of miles an hour.[151] Their bag of tricks is almost endless, but this is really nothing unexpected for spiritual beings who could intelligently and powerfully manipulate matter and energy to their own ends. Those involved in the occult have, for hundreds of years, called this process transmutation or transmogrification.[152]

However the UFO is produced, it is frequently of small dimensions—an area where an extremely large amount of energy is concentrated. (A few have been as large as ten miles in diameter.) This energy can manifest pulsed light phenomena of a variety of colors, and apparently produce electromagnetic radiation that may distort mechanical operations and/or witnesses' perceptions. Dr. Vallee states: "The clinical data that have been collected by serious investigators of the UFO phenomenon thus form an impressive body of empirical facts. Various explanations have been proposed, from magnetic fields to pulsed microwaves. They account for some of the effects, although no single explanation accounts for all the phenomena."[153]

John Keel observes that, as in the world of the occult (e.g., ectoplasmic materializations apparently drawn from the sitters in the seance circle), UFOs involve radical alterations of energy: "The statistical data . . . indicate that flying

saucers are *not* stable machines requiring fuel, mainte-
nance, and logistical support. They are, in all probability,
transmogrifications of energy and do not exist in the same
way that this book exists. They are not permanent con-
structions of matter."[154]

Dr. Kurt Wagner is a physicist whose Ph.D. degree was
taken in the field of general relativity theory. He comments:

> It seems to me likely that UFOs are large-scale viola-
> tions of the second law in which energy is arranged to
> take on enough of a force field appearance so that it
> appears to look like matter, yet it's really just an
> energy concentration—it's not really solid matter in
> the usual sense.[155]

In conclusion, although we may not be able to explain
exactly how UFOs are produced, there are more than suffi-
cient illustrations in the world of the occult to indicate that
they are produced in the same manner as spiritistic phenomena in general.

UFO experiences may be the result of induced hypnosis,
psychic projections, human or environmental vampirization
of energy (manifesting itself as heat loss, physical effects,
etc.), apparitions, physical materializations, etc.—in other
words, through intelligent manipulation of the mind and
the created order, both physical and spiritual.

Again, the demonic theory does not explain precisely
how such phenomena are produced, but neither can any
other theory. The issue it does raise is that of personal
involvement. If people are potentially involving themselves
in something evil, UFOs are better avoided.

12. What are the dangers of UFO contact?

UFOs are dangerous because they are occultic (demonic)
phenomena. The dangers that one finds in occult practices
are precisely those dangers that one encounters in contacts
with UFOs: physical injury or death, severe mental damage, and demon possession.

Dr. Jacques Vallee personally investigated some 50 cases
of visual UFO contact firsthand, meeting and interviewing
the witnesses himself. This was usually done at the site
itself, whether in the United States, Brazil, France, or
Argentina. He notes that "many of them involve secondary
physical and medical effects, including twelve cases of fatal
injuries in which the victim typically survived less than 24
hours."[156] He further observes, "If accidents are included in

the study [of hazards], along with cases in which victims are directly exposed to a hostile light, the list of deaths related to UFO cases becomes significantly longer."[157]

The abduction experience is no less dangerous. In his article "Post-Abduction Syndrome" psychologist Dr. David M. Jacobs begins by noting:

> Physically, the abduction experience can leave its victims with a wide range of aftereffects. Scars, eye problems, muscle pains, bruises, unusual vaginal and navel discharges, genital disorders, neurological problems, pregnancy anomalies, ovarian difficulties, and so forth, are just a few of the myriad of physical problems associated with abduction experiences. Physical problems can have permanent and deleterious effects on abductees. They can seriously harm a person and significantly alter the course of one's life. Although the physical effects of abductions can be extremely severe, for the purposes of this paper I am going to concentrate on the myriad of psychological difficulties that also arise in abduction victims. It is these problems that have the most destructive effect on the course of people's lives and on their relationships with others.[158]

Among the psychological consequences discussed are sleep disturbances, fears, phobias, panic disorders, obsessions, bizarre "bleed-through" memories, out-of-body contacts with the "dead," and damage to psychosexual development, especially among children.

If the UFO entities were really advanced extraterrestrials visiting us, one might expect that they would grant their host society a certain measure of respect. They would have the intellectual, technological, and moral capacity to abide by the rules of their host planet and not injure others. But this is precisely what we do not find. UFOs produce rays of light that maim, blind, and even kill people. Clearly they are in control of these outbursts of energy, for there are many such instances. All too often contactees have been lied to, misinformed, made to look like fools, or ruined psychologically. Frequently they have been driven to insanity and suicide.

Both UFOs and the entities that accompany them have in many instances injured people physically, psychologically, and spiritually, and this argues for their evil nature, not their benign nature. As Keel warns:

> Dabbling with UFOs can be as dangerous as dabbling with black magic. The phenomenon preys upon the

neurotic, the gullible, and the immature. Paranoid-schizophrenia, demonomania, and even suicide can result—and has resulted in a number of cases. A mild curiosity about UFOs can turn into a destructive obsession. For this reason, I strongly recommend that parents forbid their children from becoming involved. Schoolteachers and other adults should not encourage teen-agers to take an interest in the subject. ...People have actually died after exposure to the rays...from UFOs.[159]

Psychiatrist Dr. Berthold Schwartz comments: "All too little has been done in clinical and laboratory study of such alleged UFO-related psychic and psychological effects as anxiety and panic reactions, confusion, mood and personality changes, loss of consciousness, automatisms, amnesia, paralysis, parathesia, weakness, wasting, burns, heat sensations, eye injury, transitory blindness, hoarseness, skin lesions, reported radiation effects..." etc.[160]

Dr. Bernard E. Finch observes that the effects of relatively close UFO encounters include: headaches, dizziness, hallucinations (visual, auditory, and olfactory), dramatic emotional changes, delusions, and amnesia with psychotic features. He comments, "In several recent encounters there were symptoms of epileptiform discharge with loss of consciousness."[161]

Well-known UFO researcher Charles Bowen, referring to many cases of UFO-induced damage, including lethal incidents, counsels that it is better not to be personally involved in UFO sightings rather than to be involved and risk a "50-50 chance of something nasty happening."[162]

Brad Steiger warns, "There is a wealth of well-documented evidence that UFOs have been responsible for murders, assaults, burnings with direct-ray focus, radiation sickness, kidnappings, pursuits of automobiles, attacks on homes, disruptions of power sources, paralysis, mysterious cremations and destruction of aircraft."[163]

In his article "Why UFOs Are Hostile" Jerome Clark refers to a number of hostility cases and observes, "There are many similar cases. They usually occur in secluded areas in the darkness, and the witnesses are often paralyzed, as was Maris de Wilde, injured like Flynn or Jesus Paz, killed as were Miguel Jose Viana and Manuel Pereria de Cruz, or kidnapped like Rivlino Mafra da Silva."[164] John Keel argues that "millions of people have been affected at least temporarily by UFO contact, [and] thousands have gone insane and ended up in mental institutions after their experiences with these things begin."[165]

Unfortunately, we have not begun to catalog the damage that has been done to people who have pursued UFO phenomena. Today, a number of leading researchers are becoming much more cautious concerning the potential dangers of UFO contact. Vallee himself, after his recent trip to Brazil to investigate firsthand a large number of sightings and contacts, realized that "the UFO problem was much more dangerous . . . than the literature of the field had indicated. . . . The medical injuries consecutive to UFO encounters [are] perhaps the most significant area of investigation for the future."[166]

Unfortunately, the medical, psychiatric, and spiritual injuries have been there all along, but for unknown reasons most serious researchers seem to have refused to consider the reports.

13. Does the Bible say anything about UFOs?

Many people claim that the Bible contains stories of encounters with UFOs. They see "UFOs" in the Bible in the pillar of fire and cloud in Exodus, in Ezekiel's "wheels," in Elijah's "chariot of fire," and even in the star of Bethlehem and Christ's ascension. In essence, all the miracles of the Bible are supposedly the results of UFO intervention.

For some rationalistic-oriented theologians, UFOs have also become a means to escape the "embarrassment" of the supernatural. In other words, the miracles of the Bible are now understood as resulting from the "supertechnology" of aliens, in spite of the fact that a UFO interpretation of a given miracle may clearly be more incredible than a supernatural one! Rather than taking the text at face value in terms of its cultural and historical setting, "biblical" ufology reinterprets it in light of modern UFO sightings and disregards the text itself when it conflicts with its premises.[167]

But anyone who interprets the Bible normally will discover that the historical events in the Old Testament did not involve the activity of so-called "space gods" (as per von Daniken) but the God of the universe. Moses, Joshua, Samuel, the judges, the kings, and the prophets all knew this, as their writings testify. They knew the difference between monotheism and an idolatry of worshiping the creature, whether from outer space or not. In fact, no one who has read the Old or New Testament fairly can believe that they deal with "space beings" rather than God Himself. To accept the Bible at face value is to nullify "biblical" ufology.

The "saucer theologians"—those who see biblical religion as a product of extraterrestrial intervention—fail to realize that a portrait of extraterrestrial or UFO contact is nowhere painted in Scripture apart from their own imagination. The failure of the biblical UFO hypothesis is simply that it makes UFOs more than they can ever be. According to the biblical text, we are dealing with the actions of an infinite, unlimited being producing miraculous phenomena, not a limited physical craft producing supertechnological phenomena.

The Reverend Barry H. Downing is the author of *The Bible and Flying Saucers* (Berkeley Books, 1989). He has the Bachelor of Divinity degree from Princeton Theological Seminary and the Ph.D. degree from the University of Edinburgh. He has also had a longtime interest in UFOs, having been a consultant to the Mutual UFO Network in theology for 16 years and on the editorial staff of the MUFON UFO Journal. His personal conviction is that UFOs engineered the biblical religion and represent a divine phenomenon. He believes they come from God and "that UFOs carry the angels of God."[168] In spite of his convictions he also confesses, "I have to say that I cannot name a single theologian who thinks my theory is a good idea."[169]

Nevertheless, he believes that "the Judeo-Christian tradition can mostly be saved by going in the direction I have gone."[170] In *The Oregonian* (April 22, 1989) Dr. Downing said that confirmation of UFOs as a godly phenomenon "would not mean undermining biblical faith, but reinterpreting it in light of UFO phenomena." This, of course, is precisely the problem: Once the Bible is interpreted in light of UFO phenomena, it self-destructs theologically because the "UFO phenomenon" is itself antibiblical.

But in spite of his personal conviction that UFOs are divine, he also is forced to admit that "it might be that the UFO reality is itself fraudulent, trying to make us think it is divine."[171]

Does the Bible answer the dilemma of UFOs one way or the other? We think it does. While the Bible does not comment directly upon UFOs, it also does not comment directly upon a large number of other topics, such as abortion, euthanasia and genetic engineering. However, it does offer principles by which all of these subjects may be evaluated. Given what we know from the phenomena we are experiencing, the Bible does have a good deal to teach about the subject. If UFO phenomena are occultic, then the Bible condemns involvement with them as much as any other occultic pursuit (e.g., Deuteronomy 18:9-12). If the UFO entities give antibiblical messages, encourage the pursuit of the occult, and deny the biblical teaching on Jesus

Christ, God, salvation, biblical authority, etc., then it is incredible that a Christian can think that UFOs could be divine. Certainly the divine angels of God would never present teachings to mankind that dishonor Christ, oppose God's way of salvation, and undermine biblical truth in a dozen different categories.

In fact, in 20 years of researching this field, including reading through tens of thousands of pages of information by hundreds of authors, we have yet to find a *single* indication that UFOs or UFO entities could be divine.

Several Scriptures may have some bearing upon the UFO phenomenon. For example, the Bible teaches that in the last times Satan will come upon the world with "all power and signs and false wonders, and with all the deception of wickedness," and that God will allow great signs in the sky (2 Thessalonians 2:9,10; Luke 21:11). Thus a phenomenon like satanic UFOs might be expected as our age draws to a close. Ephesians 2:2 refers to Satan when it speaks of "the prince of the *power* of the *air*." In the original Greek text the word "power" (*exousia*) is a collective term meaning the whole empire of evil spirits, and the term "air" (*aer*) means the lower atmosphere, physical air in the normal sense. The demonic center of power, according to this text, is the lower atmosphere around the earth. If the air is the region of the demons' might, we can see the UFO interconnection that could exist. Scripture says we war "against the spiritual forces of wickedness *in the heavenly places*" (Ephesians 6:12). All in all, everything one would expect of spiritual warfare and deception can be found in the UFO phenomena.

Satan is described as being "the god of this world" (2 Corinthians 4:4), "the ruler of this world" (John 16:11), and the deceiver of the nations (Revelation 20:3). We are also told that "the whole world lies in the power of the evil one" (1 John 5:19).

In conclusion, we see no evidence at all that the UFO phenomenon can be considered either divine or biblical.

4. How does one find deliverance from the consequences of occult involvement resulting from UFO contact?

However they have done so, those who have become associated with UFOs and their entities have become involved with lying spirits which the Bible identifies as demons. There is one, and only one, way of release—through the power of Jesus Christ. Individuals seeking deliverance should confess their sin, renounce all involvement in this area, and wholeheartedly turn their lives over to Christ. They should also seek counsel from a local pastor who is committed to Christ and should request prayer for their particular situation. In our *Facts On the Occult* we have listed specific helps for those seeking escape from occult bondage. Those who do sincerely turn to Jesus Christ in true repentance and faith *will* find deliverance. There may be a battle, but it will be won!

If you are involved with UFO entities or other aspects of the occult, we suggest the following prayer:

> Lord Jesus Christ, *I humbly acknowledge* that I have sinned in my thinking, speaking and acting, that I am guilty of deliberate wrongdoing, that my sins have separated me from Your Holy presence.
>
> *I firmly believe* that You died on the cross for my sins, bearing them in Your own body and suffering in my place the condemnation they deserved.
>
> *I have thoughtfully counted the cost of following You.* I sincerely repent, turning away from my past sins. I surrender to You as my Lord and Master.
>
> *So now I come to You.* I believe You have been patiently waiting for me to come to You. Lord Jesus, be my Savior and Lord forever. Amen.[15]

Please write to us at The John Ankerberg Show and we will send you information on growing in the Christian life.

CONCLUSION

We believe that the lack of evidence for the extraterrestrial hypothesis and the failure of all other theories to adequately explain UFOs require that the demonic theory not be ignored. This theory is bolstered by the harmful physical, psychological, and spiritual effects of UFO encounters, possession cases, false gospels, and much more. Consider the unethical and unbiblical orientation of the UFO entities and their teachings, their bizarre behavior and the scores of undeniable occult and demonic correlations. Consider also the innumerable close encounters that are deliberately staged events for the benefit of the viewers which suggest a plan to deceive. Their "earth" orientation historically and the fact that all UFO phenomena are consistent with the demonic theory indicate that this explanation is the best possible answer for the solution to the UFO mystery.

Notes

1. Dr. J. Allen Hynek estimates there are some 100 sitings a night somewhere around the world. See J. Allen Hynek and Jacques Vallee, *The Edge of Reality* (Chicago: Henry Regnery Company, 1975), p. 22.
2. J. Allen Hynek in *New West Magazine*, Nov. 7, 1977, p. 24.
3. According to personal correspondence with Dr. David Sanders of the University of Chicago, a computer analysis of almost 50,000 UFO sittings from 1947-1974 shows that every 61 months UFOs increase their activity, moving across the globe from a west-to-east direction in 1500-to-2000-mile leaps.
4. Jacques Vallee, *The Invisible College* (New York: Dutton, 1975), p. 207.
5. Timothy Good, *Above Top Secret: The Worldwide UFO Cover-up* (New York: Morrow, 1988), pp. 306-444.
6. Ibid., Chapter 17.
7. Interview on French radio published in *Flying Saucer Review* (FSR), Vol. 20, No. 2, pp. 3-4. See note 12.
8. Good, *Above*, p. 12.
9. E.g., *Time* magazine, Nov. 11, 1991; Gallup poll for Aug. 6, 1990.
10. Bud Hopkins, *Missing Time* (New York: Ballantine, 1988), p. 9.
11. France-Inter broadcast, Feb. 24, 1974 (interviewed by J.C. Bourret), cited in Hynek and Vallee, *The Edge*, p. 58.
12. J. Allen Hynek and Jacques Vallee, *The Edge of Reality* (Chicago: Henry Regnery Company, 1975), p. 1.
13. Ibid., p. 240.
14. Jacques Vallee, *Confrontations: A Scientist's Search for Alien Contact* (New York: Ballantine, 1991), pp. 216-18.
15. Thanks to Jon Van Hemelryck, Paia, Maui, Hawaii.
16. Vallee, *Confrontations*, p. 159.
17. Whitley Strieber, *Transformation: The Breakthrough* (New York: Morrow, 1988), p. 9.
18. Vallee, *Confrontations*, p. 12.
19. Jacques Vallee, *Messengers of Deception: UFO Contacts and Cults* (Berkeley, CA: And Or Press, 1979), pp. 9-10.
20. *The Skeptical Inquirer*, Fall 1987, p. 14.
21. *Chattanooga News–Free Press*, Dec. 8, 1991.
22. David Swift, "A Sociologist's Reaction," in Vallee, *Messengers*, p. 229.
23. Vallee, *Messengers*, p. 9.
24. Ibid., p. 19.
25. Ibid., pp. 20-21.
26. Ibid.
27. Official policy statement found in FSR descriptive brochure, 1992 (FSR, P.O. Box 162, High Wycombe, Bucks, HP13 5D2 England).
28. Charles Bowen, "Behind the Times," in *Flying Saucer Review*, Vol. 20, No. 2, p. 2.
29. E.g., Major Donald Keyhoe, *Aliens from Space* (New York: Signet, 1974), p. 242.
30. John Weldon and Zola Levitt, *UFOs: What on Earth Is Happening?* (New York: Bantam, 1976), Appendix 4.
31. Cf. Jacques Vallee, *Passport to Magonia: From Folklore to Flying Saucers* (Chicago: Henry Regnery), 1969.
32. E.g., Dr. Aime Michael's extrapolation from Sturrock's study, "UFO Reports from AIAA Members," in *Astronautics and Aeronautics*, May 1974, p. 60.
33. Vallee, *Confrontations*, p. 14.
34. Ibid., p. 131; e.g., *Flying Saucer Review*, *MUFON Journal*, and other reputable periodicals have carried many articles on this over the years.
35. E.g., Ivan Sanderson, *Uninvited Visitors* (New York: Cowels, 1969), p. 176.
36. M.K. Jessup, *The Expanding Case for the UFO* (New York: Citadel, 1957), pp. 16-17.
37. Cited in Hayden Hewes, "Blue Book Files Released," in *Canadian UFO Report*, Vol. 4, No. 4, 1977, p. 20.
38. *New York Times Book Review*, July 27, 1975.
39. Billy Graham, *Angels* (Boston: G.K. Hall, 1976), pp. 12,16.
40. Ibid., p. 21.
41. Clifford Wilson and John Weldon, *Close Encounters: A Better Explanation* (San Diego: Master Books, 1978), Chapters 8, 9, 10, Appendix A, passim.
42. E.g., Berthold Schwartz, interview in *UFO Report*, Oct. 1976, p. 28; Clifford Wilson, *The Alien Agenda* (New York: Signet, 1988), p. 179; Clark and Coleman, *The Unidentified* (New York: Warner, 1975), p. 236; Brad Steiger, *The Aquarian Revelations* (New York: Dell, 1971), p. 58; Trevor James, *They Live in the Sky* (Los Angeles: New Age Publishing, 1958), p. 25; Martin Ebon, ed., *The Amazing Uri Geller* (New York: Signet, 1975), p. 131.
43. Francis Barret, *The Magus*, Book II (New York: University Books, 1801, 1967), pp. 48-54.
44. Ibid.
45. G.H. Pember, *Earth's Earliest Ages and Their Connection with Modern Spiritualism and Theosophy* (Old Tappan, NJ: Revel, n.d.), p. 254.

46. Augustine, *The City of God*, Book 18, Chapter 5, cited in Philip Schaff, ed., *Nicene and Post-Nicene Fathers*, Vol. 2, First Series (Grand Rapids: Eerdmans, 1970), p. 364.
47. In *The APRO* [Aerial Phenomena Research Organization] *Bulletin* (Tucson, AZ), Feb. 1976.
48. Vallee, *Confrontations*, p. 204.
49. Among them Dr. J. Allen Hynek and many authors in the pages of the FSR.
50. Raymond E. Fowler, *The Watchers: The Secret Design Behind UFO Abduction* (New York: Bantam, 1991), pp. xv, 183.
51. Vallee, *Confrontations*, p. 89.
52. Lynn Catoe, *UFOs and Related Subjects: An Annotated Bibliography* (Washington D.C.: U.S. Government Printing Office, 1969), p. iv (prepared under Air Force Office of Scientific Research Project Order 67-0002 and 68-0003).
53. Pierre Guerin, "Thirty Years After Kenneth Arnold," in *Flying Saucer Review*, Vol. 25, No. 1, p. 13.
54. Ibid., p. 14.
55. Ibid.
56. Ibid.
57. John A. Keel, *UFOs: Operation Trojan Horse* (New York: Putnam's, 1970), p. 215.
58. Ibid., p. 299.
59. Trevor James, "The Case for Contact—Part Two," in *Flying Saucer Review*, Vol. 8, No. 1, p. 10.
60. David Stupple and William McNeece, "Contactees, Cults and Culture," in *1979 MUFON UFO Symposium Proceedings*, p. 49.
61. Vallee, *Messengers*, p. 15.
62. Ibid., p. 19.
63. Vallee, *Invisible*, pp. 3,201,204.
64. Vallee, *Confrontations*, p. 13.
65. Ibid., p. 146.
66. Ibid., p. 159.
67. Ibid., pp. 160-61.
68. Vallee, *Messengers*, p. 222.
69. Ivar MacKay, "UFO Entities: Occult and Physical," in *Flying Saucer Review*, Vol. 19, No. 2, p. 28.
70. Ivar MacKay, "UFOs and the Occult" (2 parts), in *Flying Saucer Review*, Vol. 16, Nos. 4 & 5.
71. Kenneth Ring and Christopher Rosing, "The Omega Project: A Psychological Survey of Persons Reporting Abductions and Other UFO Encounters," in *Journal of UFO Studies*, New Series, Vol. 2, 1990, p. 59.
72. Ibid., p. 71.
73. Ibid., p. 76.
74. Ibid., p. 77.
75. Ibid., p. 81; cf. pp. 79-80.
76. Ibid., pp. 86-87.
77. Ibid., p. 93.
78. Hundreds of examples can be found in *Flying Saucer Review*, 1955-1992.
79. Strieber, *Communion: A True Story* (New York: Morrow, 1987), pp. 35,274,282.
80. Ibid., pp. 25-26.
81. Ibid., pp. 108-09.
82. Ibid., pp. 93-95.
83. Ibid., p. 131; cf. p. 104 for the smell of sulfur.
84. Ibid., p. 136.
85. Strieber, *Transformation*, p. 96.
86. Ibid., pp. 44-45.
87. Ibid., p. 123.
88. Ibid.
89. Ibid., p. 172.
90. Ibid., p. 181.
91. Ibid., p. 183.
92. Ibid., p. 184.
93. Strieber, *Communion*, pp. 64-65,96.
94. Ibid., p. 273.
95. Strieber, *Transformation*, p. 10.
96. Strieber, *Communion*, p. 260.
97. Stuart Goldman, "They're Here!" (manuscript letter sent to John Weldon on Nov. 29, 1989).
98. Ibid.
99. Ibid.
100. Janet Gregory, "Similarities in UFO and Demon Lore," in *Flying Saucer Review*, Vol. 17, No. 2, p. 32.
101. Jonathan Caplan, " 'Parallelism' As a Terminology," in *Flying Saucer Review*, Vol. 20, No. 3, p. 22.
102. Clark and Coleman, *The Unidentified*, p. 236.
103. Brad Steiger, *The Aquarian Revelations*, p. 58.

104. Trevor James, *They Live in the Sky*, p. 25.
105. Bryant and Helen Reeve, *Flying Saucer Pilgrimage* (Amherst, WI: Amherst Press, 1957).
106. Robert S. Ellwood, Jr., *Religious and Spiritual Groups in Modern America* (Englewood Cliffs, NJ: Prentice Hall, 1973), pp. 131,134.
107. Robert S. Ellwood, Jr., "Religious Movements and UFOs," in Ronald Story, ed., *The Encyclopedia of UFOs* (New York: Dolphin, 1980), p. 307.
108. E.g., see the following articles: "Apparitions," "Chemical Phenomena," "Clairvoyance," "Dematerializations," "Ectoplasm," "Electric Phenomena," "Hauntings," "Light," "Luminous Phenomena," "Magnetic Phenomena," "Materializations," "Matter Passing Through Matter," "Mediumism," "Movement," "Planetary Travels," "Poltergeists," "Psychic Force," "Spirits of the Living," "Thoughtforms," "Touches," "Trances," "Transfiguration," "Transportation."
109. Martin Ebon, ed., *Amazing*, p. 131.
110. Keel, *Operation*, pp. 239-42; *FSR Special Issue* No. 2, p. 17.
111. Vallee, *Confrontations*, p. 216; cf. *Fifth APRO UFO Symposium*, p. 18.
112. Keel, *Our Haunted Planet* (Greenwich, CT: Fawcett, 1971), p. 218.
113. See our *The Facts on the Occult*, and references.
114. Keel, *Haunted*, pp. 128,162; Keel, *Trojan Horse*, pp. 45,199,215,220,244-46,252, 270-71,290, etc.; Steiger, *Aquarian*, p. 86; Eric Norman, *Gods and Devils from Outer Space*, p. 120; B.E. Schwartz, *FSR*, Vol. 20, No. 1, pp. 3-11; Reeve, *Flying Saucer Pilgrimage*, p. 128.
115. E.g., Reeve, *Flying Saucer*, pp. 9,92,95,164; Clark and Coleman, *The Unidentified*, pp. 203-12; Keel, *Haunted*, p. 128.
116. E.g., examples are found in Steiger, *Aquarian*; cf. The Academy of Atlantis in Los Angeles.
117. E.g., Brad Steiger, "UFO Contactees: Heralds of the New Age," in *UFO Universe*, Summer 1989, No. 6.
118. Brad Steiger and Hayden Hewes, *UFO Missionaries Extraordinary* (New York: Pocket Books, 1976), p. 63.
119. E.A.I. Mackay, "UFO Entities: Occult and Physical," in *Flying Saucer Review*, Vol. 19, No. 2, p. 27.
120. Keel, *Operation*, p. 183.
121. E.g., Vallee, *Messengers*, p. 219; Forrest Crawford, "The Revealing Science of Ufology: An Anatomy of Abduction Correlations," in *MUFON: UFO Journal*, Dec. 1991, p. 15.
122. Alvin Lawson, "Alien Roots: Six UFO Entity Types and Some Possible Earthly Ancestors," in *1979 MUFON Symposium Proceedings*, pp. 152-71; Jacques Vallee, *Passport to Magonia*, passim.
123. Lawson, "Alien Roots," p. 162.
124. G.N.M. Tyrrell, *Apparitions* (New York: Collier, 1963 rev.), Chapter 2.
125. Ibid., pp. 76,66,86.
126. Ibid., p. 63.
127. Ibid., p. 76.
128. Ibid., p. 65.
129. Ibid., p. 102.
130. Martin Luther, *Commentary on Galatians*, Chapter 3, Verse 1 (Westwood, NJ: Revell, n.d.), p. 190; Some eds. do not contain this phrasing.
131. Andrija Puharich, *Uri* (New York: Bantam, 1975), p. 112.
132. Jon Klimo, *Channeling: Investigations on Receiving Information from Paranormal Sources* (Los Angeles: Tarcher, 1987), p. 304; Robert Leichtman, "Clairvoyant Diagnosis," in *Journal of Holistic Health* (San Diego: Mandala Society, 1977), p. 40; Robert Leichtman, *Eileen Garrett Returns* (Columbus, OH: Ariel Press, 1984), pp. 46-48; Robert Leichtman and Carl Japiske, *The Art of Living*, Vol. 4 (Columbus, OH: Ariel Press, 1984), p. 78; Arthur Guirdham, *A Foot in Both Worlds* (London, Neville: Spearman, 1973), p. 219; Albert Villoldo and Stanley Krippner, *Healing States: A Journal into the World of Spiritual Healing and Shamanism* (New York: Simon & Schuster, 1987), p. 18.
133. Hopkins, *Missing*, pp. 7-8.
134. Vallee, *Confrontations*, p. 142.
135. E.g., *Science*, Oct. 14, 1983, pp. 184-85 and June 4, 1988; *Wall Street Journal*, Mar. 2, 1988; Vallee, *Confrontations*, pp. 142-43,156-58.
136. Vallee, *Confrontations*, p. 158; cf. the critiques of hypnosis use in UFO "Abductions" in *The Skeptical Inquirer*, Vol. 5, No. 3; Vol. 12, Nos. 2 & 3.
137. Lawson, "Alien Roots," p. 166; cf. Lawson, "What Can We Learn from Hypnosis of Imaginary Abductees?" in *1977 MUFON Symposium Proceedings*, p. 166.
138. Lawson, ibid., in *1977 MUFON Proceedings*, p. 107.
139. Vallee, *Confrontations*, p. 158.
140. John Rimmer, *The Evidence for Alien Abductions* (Wellingborough, North Hamptonshire: The Aquarium Press, 1984), p. 152.
141. Ann Druffel, "Hypnotic Regression of UFO Abductees," in *Flying Saucer Review*, Vol. 25, No. 5, p. 31.
142. E.g., Raphael Gasson, *The Challenging Counterfeit* (Plainfield, NJ: Logos, 1969).

143. John Ankerberg et. al., *One World: Bible Prophecy and the New World Order* (Chicago: Moody Press, 1991).
144. *Los Angeles Times*, Aug. 22, 1975; cf. the statement by General Douglas MacArthur in *The UFO Reporter*, Mar./Apr. 1975, p. 7; *New York Times*, Oct. 7, 1955; cf. W.J. Brown, *Flying Saucer Review*, Sep./Oct. 1955.
145. Vallee, *Messengers*, pp. 218-19. Cf. Brad Steiger's *The Fellowship*.
146. E.g., Richard Haines in *Journal of Scientific Exploration*, Vol. 1, No. 2 (1987).
147. Kehoe, *Aliens*, p. 242.
148. E.g., George C. Andrews, *Extra-Terrestrials Among Us* (St. Paul, MN: Llewellyn, 1987), pp. 2-6; cf. *Flying Saucer Review* issues.
149. Ibid., p. 4; cf. *FSR* issues, 1955-1992.
150. Ibid.
151. Ibid.
152. Keel, *Operation*, p. 57.
153. Vallee, *Confrontations*, p. 110.
154. Keel, *Operation*, p. 182.
155. Kurt Wagner, "Interview with David Fetcho," in *SCP Journal*, Vol. 1, No. 2, Aug. 1977, p. 20.
156. Vallee, *Confrontations*, p. 15.
157. Ibid., p. 113.
158. David M. Jacobs, "Abductions and the ET Hypothesis," in *MUFON, 1988 International Symposium Proceedings: Abductions and the E.T. Hypothesis*, p. 87.
159. Keel, *Operation*, p. 220.
160. Berthold Schwartz in *Canadian UFO Report*, Vol. 1, No. 8, Fall 1970.
161. Bernard E. Finch, "Beware the Saucers," in *Flying Saucer Review*, Vol. 12, No. 1, p. 5
162. Charles Bowen, "Mail Bag," in *Flying Saucer Review*, Vol. 19, No. 5, p. 27.
163. Brad Steiger, *Flying Saucers Are Hostile* (New York: Award, 1976), p. 8.
164. Jerome Clark, "Why UFOs Are Hostile," in *Flying Saucer Review*, Vol. 13, No. 6, p. 19.
165. John Keel, *Strange Creatures from Time and Space* (Greenwich, CT: Fawcett, 1970), p. 189.
166. Vallee, *Confrontations*, pp. 17-18.
167. For critiques of R.L. Dione's *God Drives a Flying Saucer*, Dr. Barry Downing's *The Bible and Flying Saucers*, and Joseph Blumrich's *The Spaceships of Ezekiel*, see John Weldon and Clifford Wilson, *Close Encounters*, Appendix C.
168. Barry Downing, "E.T. Contact: The Religious Dimension," in *MUFON 1990 International UFO Symposium Proceedings; UFOs: The Impact of E.T. Contact Upon Society*, p. 54.
169. Ibid.
170. Ibid., p. 55.
171. Ibid., p. 59.